# Read and Succeed:
# Comprehension

**Consultant**

Mary Rosenberg, M.A.Ed.

SHELL EDUCATION

## Contributing Author

Jennifer Kroll

## Publishing Credits

Dona Herweck Rice, *Editor-in-Chief*; Lee Aucoin, *Creative Director*; Don Tran, *Print Production Manager;* Timothy J. Bradley, *Illustration Manager*; Conni Medina, M.A.Ed., *Editorial Director*; Kristy Stark, M.A.Ed., *Editor*; Stephanie Reid, *Cover Designer*; Robin Erickson, *Interior Layout Designer;* Corinne Burton, M.S.Ed., *Publisher*

Copyright 2004 McREL. www.mcrel.org/standards-benchmarks.

## Shell Education

5301 Oceanus Drive
Huntington Beach, CA  92649-1030
http://www.shelleducation.com

### ISBN 978-1-4258-0724-5

©2010 Shell Educational Publishing, Inc.
Reprinted 2012

# Table of Contents

# Introduction

Comprehension is the goal of every reading task. The *Read and Succeed: Comprehension* series can help lay the foundation of comprehension skills that are essential for a lifetime of learning. The series was written specifically to provide the purposeful practice students need in order to succeed in reading comprehension. The more students practice, the more confident and capable they can become.

## Why You Need This Book

- **It is standards based**. The skill practice pages are aligned to the Mid-continent Research for Education and Learning (McREL) standards. (See page 7.)
- **It has focused lessons**. Each practice page covers a key comprehension skill. Skills are addressed multiple times to provide several opportunities for mastery.
- **It employs advanced organization**. Having students encounter the question page first gives them a "heads up" when they approach the text, thereby enhancing comprehension and promoting critical-thinking abilities.
- **It has appropriate reading levels**. All passages have a grade level calculated based on the Shell Education leveling system, which was developed under the guidance of Dr. Timothy Rasinski, along with the staff at Shell Education.
- **It has an interactive whiteboard-compatible Teacher Resource CD.** This can be used to enhance instruction and support literacy skills.

## How to Use This Book

First, determine what sequence will best benefit your students. Work through the book in order (as the skills become progressively more difficult) to cover all key skills. For reinforcement of specific skills, select skills as needed.

Then determine what instructional setting you will use. See below for suggestions for a variety of instructional settings:

| Whole-Class or Small-Group Instruction | Independent Practice or Centers | Homework |
|---|---|---|
| Read and discuss the Skill Focus. Write the name of the skill on the board. | Create a folder for each student. Include a copy of the selected skill practice page and passage. | Give each student a copy of the selected skill practice page and passage. |
| Read and discuss responses to each question. Read the text when directed (as a group, in pairs, or individually). | Have students complete the skill practice page. Remind them to begin by reading the Skill Focus and to read the passage when directed. | Have students complete the skill practice page. Remind them to begin by reading the Skill Focus and to read the passage when directed. |
| Read and discuss the Critical Thinking question. Allow time for discussion before having students write their responses. | Collect the skill practice pages and check students' answers. Or, provide each student with a copy of the answer key (pages 138–149). | Collect the skill practice pages and check students' answers. Or, provide each student with a copy of the answer key (pages 138–149). |

# Research Support for the
## *Read and Succeed: Comprehension* Series

Comprehension is the ability to derive meaning from text. It is critically important not only for the development of children's reading skills but also for students' abilities to obtain a complete education. The National Reading Panel (2000) states that comprehension is an active process that requires an intentional interaction between the reader and the text. A reader must engage in problem-solving thinking processes in order to relate the ideas represented in print to his or her own knowledge and experiences and build mental images to store in memory.

**Teaching students to use specific strategies can improve their comprehension.** To some degree, readers acquire such strategies informally. However, the National Reading Panel confirmed that explicit instruction in comprehension strategies is highly effective in enhancing understanding. That's why the *Read and Succeed: Comprehension* series was created: to make teaching comprehension strategies simple and time efficient. This book teaches specific strategies students can use to help them understand what they are reading.

**Having students know in advance the questions they will be asked helps them to attend to the material.** It gives them a focus as they read. It helps them to look for clues and to identify information they will need to remember. But most importantly, it allows them to organize information in their minds, building neural pathways that will be used again and again. Essentially, having a focus as they read teaches children how to think. This is why the skill practice page always appears before the reading passage in *Read and Succeed: Comprehension*.

**Teaching a combination of reading comprehension techniques is the most effective approach for instruction.** When students use strategies appropriately, they can improve their recall, question answering, question generation, and summarization of texts. Also, used in combination, these techniques can improve results in standardized comprehension tests. Yet teaching reading comprehension strategies to students at all grade levels can be complex. The *Read and Succeed: Comprehension* series was designed to make this process straightforward. Each book contains 65 lessons. Each lesson has a specific focus to concentrate on an important reading skill for a fiction or a nonfiction text. Step by step, students will learn the grade-level-appropriate skills they need to read and understand a wide variety of texts.

Each skill activity is independent; they need not be done in a certain order. However, it is in students' best interest to complete all of the activities. Using the *Read and Succeed: Comprehension* series will save you time and effort while simultaneously providing students with the vital skills needed to achieve 21st century comprehension and critical-thinking skills.

---

National Institute of Child Health and Human Development. 2000. *Report of the National Reading Panel. Teaching children to read: An evidence-based assessment of the scientific research literature on reading and its implications for reading instruction* (NIH Publication No. 00-4769). Washington, DC: U.S. Government Printing Office.

# Standards Correlations

Shell Education is committed to producing educational materials that are research and standards based. In this effort, we have correlated all of our products to the academic standards of all 50 states, the District of Columbia, and the Department of Defense Dependent Schools.

## How to Find Standards Correlations

To print a customized correlation report of this product for your state, visit our website at **www.shelleducation.com** and follow the on-screen directions. If you require assistance in printing correlation reports, please contact Customer Service at 1-877-777-3450.

## Purpose and Intent of Standards

The No Child Left Behind legislation mandates that all states adopt academic standards that identify the skills students will learn in kindergarten through grade twelve. While many states had already adopted academic standards prior to NCLB, the legislation set requirements to ensure the standards were detailed and comprehensive.

Standards are designed to focus instruction and guide adoption of curricula. Standards are statements that describe the criteria necessary for students to meet specific academic goals. They define the knowledge, skills, and content students should acquire at each level. Standards are also used to develop standardized tests to evaluate students' academic progress.

Teachers are required to demonstrate how their lessons meet state standards. State standards are used in development of all of our products, so educators can be assured they meet the academic requirements of each state.

## McREL Compendium

We use the Mid-continent Research for Education and Learning (McREL) Compendium to create standards correlations. Each year, McREL analyzes state standards and revises the compendium. By following this procedure, McREL is able to produce a general compilation of national standards. Each lesson in this product is based on one or more McREL standards. The chart on the following page lists each standard taught in this product and the page numbers for the corresponding lessons.

# McREL Correlations Chart

| Skill | Skill Focus and Page Numbers |
|---|---|
| Uses mental images based on pictures and print to comprehend text | *Mental Images*, 20–21, 22–23, 24–25; *Graphics*, 74–75, 76–77, 78–79 |
| Uses meaning clues (e.g., pictures, captions, title, cover, headings, story structure, story topic) to aid comprehension and make predictions about content (e.g., action, events, character's behavior) | *Preview*, 8–9, 10–11, 12–13; *Predict*, 14–15, 16–17, 18–19; *Title and Headings*, 62–63, 64–65, 66–67; *Typeface and Captions*, 68–69, 70–71, 72–73 |
| Understands a variety of literary passages and texts | **Applies to all stories in the book** |
| Knows setting, main characters, main events, sequence, and problems in stories | *Setting*, 44–45, 46–47, 48–49; *Plot*, 50–51, 52–53, 54–55; *Characters*, 56–57, 58–59, 60–61; *Time Order*, 96–97, 98–99, 100–101; *Logical Order*, 102–103, 104–105, 106–107 |
| Knows the main idea of a story | *Main Idea*, 80–81, 82–83, 84–85; *Main Idea and Details*, 92–93, 94–95 |
| Relates stories to personal experiences (e.g., events, characters, conflicts, themes) | *Ask Questions*, 32–33, 34–35, 36–37; *Make Connections*, 38–39, 40–41, 42–43 |
| Understands a variety of informational texts | **Applies to all nonfiction texts in the book**<br><br>*Time Order*, 96–97, 98–99, 100–101; *Logical Order*, 102–103, 104–105, 106–107; *Cause and Effect*, 114–115, 116–117; *Compare and Contrast*, 118–119, 120–121 |
| Uses the various parts of a book to locate information | *Table of Contents*, 126–127, 128–129; *Index*, 130–131, 132–133; *Glossary*, 134–135, 136–137 |
| Understands the main idea and supporting details of simple expository information | *Main Idea*, 80–81, 82–83, 84–85; *Details*, 86–87, 88–89, 90–91; *Main Idea and Details*, 92–93, 94–95 |
| Summarizes information found in texts (e.g., retells in own words) | *Retell*, 108–109, 110–111, 112–113 |
| Relates new information to prior knowledge and experiences | *Prior Knowledge*, 26–27, 28–29, 30–31; *Author's Purpose*, 122–123, 124–125 |

# Preview

*Before you read, look at the title and pictures. This will help you know what you will read and learn.*

1. Look at the title of the story. Look at the picture. What will you read about?

   _____

2. What do you know about this topic? Write three facts below.

   _____

   _____

   _____

3. Read the story. Write two things you learned.

   _____

   _____

**Critical Thinking**

How does previewing help you read a story?

   _____

   _____

   _____

# Brad's Kittens

Brad's cat had six kittens. The kittens were born early in the morning. They are all black and white. Some of them have white paws.

Brad held a kitten. The kitten was so tiny. It was the size of his hand! The kittens still had their eyes closed. They made tiny mewing sounds. They will stay with their mother. She will keep the kittens warm and safe.

# Preview

*Before you read, look at the title and pictures. This will help you know what you will read and learn.*

1. Read the title. Look at the picture. What will you read about?

   _____

2. Write three facts about horses.

   _____

   _____

   _____

3. Read the text. Write two things you learned.

   _____

   _____

**Critical Thinking**

Think about wild horses and pet horses. What is different about where they live?

_____

_____

_____

# All About Horses

Horses live all over the world. In the wild, they live on plains. With people, they may live in fields, stables, and corrals.

Horses are active. So, they are big eaters. They eat plants. They like grasses and grains. They like sweet treats, such as apples. They like sugar cubes, too.

A stallion is a male horse. A female horse is a mare. Horse babies are colts if they are male. They are fillies if they are female. All horse babies are called foals.

stallion

# Preview

*Before you read, look at the title and pictures. This will help you know what you will read and learn.*

1.  Read the title. Look at the picture. What will you read about?

    _____

2.  How can previewing the text help you understand what you will be reading?

    _____

    _____

3.  Read the text. Write a sentence about what you have learned.

    _____

    _____

## Critical Thinking

If there were no maps, how would people get from one city to another?

_____

_____

_____

# What Is a Map?

A map is a picture. It shows us a place. The place can be anywhere! A map can be drawn of your room. A map can be drawn of your street or school. A map can show your city or country. A map can show our world or solar system. A map can show us what it looks like under the ocean. We can make a map of a pretend world, too.

# Predict

*A prediction is a guess. You use what you know and what you have just read to make a prediction.*

1. Read the title. Look at the picture. What do you think will happen in this story?

   _____

   _____

2. Read the story. How did Thomas try to make the tooth fall out?

   _____

   _____

3. What do you think Thomas will do with his tooth?

   _____

   _____

Critical Thinking

Pretend that Mom had given Thomas applesauce. Would the tooth have fallen out? Explain.

_____

_____

_____

# The Loose Tooth

Thomas has a loose tooth. Thomas uses his tongue to wiggle the loose tooth. The tooth does not fall out.

Thomas uses his finger to wiggle the loose tooth. The tooth still does not fall out.

Thomas is sad. He is sad because the loose tooth will not fall out. Mom gives Thomas a big, shiny, fat, red apple. Thomas takes a big, big bite. Out comes Thomas's loose tooth. Only it is not loose anymore. Now it is lost! He smiles, and there is a big gap where his tooth used to be—out at last!

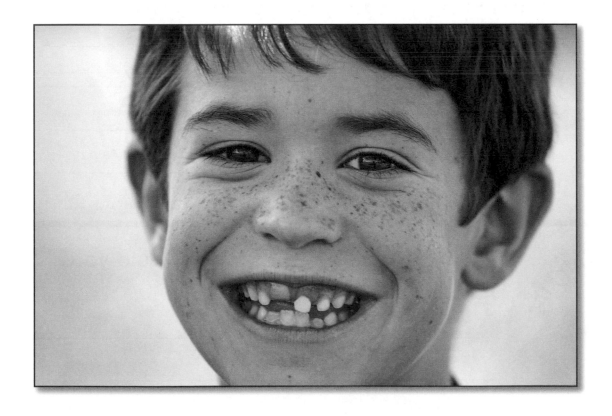

# Predict

*A prediction is a guess. You use what you know and what you have just read to make a prediction.*

1. What is a wish?

   _____

   _____

2. What do you think Liz will wish for?

   _____

   _____

3. Read the story. Have you ever had a wish come true? Tell about it.

   _____

   _____

   _____

**Critical Thinking**

If you had three wishes, what would you wish for?

   _____

   _____

   _____

# Liz's Wishes

A rock fell from the sky. It hit Liz on the head.

Liz rubbed her head. She picked up the rock.

The rock was hard and blue. It began to shake and jump. "This must be a magic rock!" said Liz.

Liz made a wish. Poof! There was a big crown. She put the crown on.

Liz made a second wish. Poof! There was a pretty, yellow gown. She put the gown on.

Liz made another wish. Poof! There was a coach. She got into the coach and rode home.

# Predict

*A prediction is a guess. You use what you know and what you have just read to make a prediction.*

1. Read the title. Read the first paragraph. Why could Sir Robert be tired?

   _____

2. Read the rest of the story. What do you think the king wanted Sir Robert to do? Draw a picture. Write a sentence about the picture.

   ```



   ```

   _____

**Critical Thinking**

What might happen to Sir Robert at the castle?

_____

_____

_____

# Sir Robert

It was nearly dark.  Sir Robert was cold.  His tired horse stumbled over rocks and roots.  Sir Robert did not want to fail the king.  But he could not keep going much farther.

All of a sudden, Sir Robert saw a light.  He pushed his tired horse on.  A few minutes later, he came riding out of the woods.  Up ahead was a castle.

# Mental Images

*As you read a text, make pictures in your mind. This will help you understand as you are reading.*

1. Read the title. Draw a picture of what you think the text will be about.

2. Read the text. Draw a picture of a sea star eating.

**Critical Thinking**

Why do you think the sea star's mouth is on the bottom of its body instead of on the top?

_____

_____

_____

# Snacking with Sea Stars

Sea stars eat in a very strange way. The sea star's mouth is on the bottom of its body. The mouth is at the middle of the star. A sea star can push its stomach out through its mouth. It turns its stomach inside out to do this. The sea star puts its stomach around a fish. It digests part of the fish. Then it pulls its stomach back into its body.

the sea star's mouth

# Mental Images

*As you read a text, make pictures in your mind. This will help you understand as you are reading.*

1. Read the title. Look at the picture. Think about what happens at a tea party.

2. Read the first paragraph. Draw a picture of the characters. Write a sentence about the picture.

```



```

_____

_____

**Critical Thinking**

Next week, Beth and her friends will have another tea party. Write about what Beth and her friends will do.

_____

_____

_____

# Tea Anyone?

Beth is having a tea party. Cat, Dog, Hen, and Bear come to the party.

Beth and her friends sit at a small table. She gives each friend a small cup. Each cup has tea in it. Beth drops a cube of sugar into each cup.

Beth gives each friend a cupcake.

Beth and her friends have a good time at the tea party. Maybe next week, they will have another tea party. Beth will invite more friends.

# Mentallmages

*As you read a text, make pictures in your mind. This will help you understand as you are reading.*

1. Read the title. Look at the picture. Write a sentence about a goal.

   _____

2. Read the story. Draw a picture of what happened. Write a sentence about the picture.

   ┌─────────────────────────────────────────┐
   │                                         │
   │                                         │
   │                                         │
   │                                         │
   │                                         │
   └─────────────────────────────────────────┘

   _____

Critical Thinking

Pretend that Sid had not scored a goal. What might have happened?

_____

_____

_____

# Goal!

Whoosh! Sid sailed down the ice on his skates. He saw that he had a clear shot and took aim. Whack! The puck went soaring past the goalie and into the net. The people in the stands jumped to their feet, clapping and cheering.

Sid looked through the crowd until he spotted his mom. She smiled brightly and gave him a thumbs up. Sid was so proud to have made his first goal of the hockey season.

# Prior Knowledge

*Before you read a text, think about what you know about that topic. This will help you understand what you read.*

1. Read the title. What birds have you seen? List them below.

   _____

   _____

2. Write two facts that you already know about birds.

   _____

   _____

3. Read the text. Write two new facts you learned about birds.

   _____

   _____

   _____

*Critical Thinking*

If you were a bird, which bird would you be? Why?

   _____

   _____

   _____

# Bird Talk

Birds are the only animals with feathers. Birds can have colorful or dull feathers.

Birds have two legs. Some birds can walk. Some birds can hop. Some birds can stand on one leg!

Birds have wings. Some birds can fly. Some birds cannot fly.

Birds have beaks. Birds may use their beaks to pick up food or to open nuts or seeds. Birds may also use their beaks to catch fish or to carry things.

Birds lay eggs. The birds lay eggs in the nest. The mother or father bird sits on the eggs to keep them warm.

# Prior Knowledge

*Before you read a text, think about what you know about that topic. This will help you understand what you read.*

1.  Read the title. Look at the picture. Make a list of animals that live on a farm.

   _____

   _____

2.  Read the story. Draw a picture to show one of the farm animals.

   ┌─────────────────────────────────────────────┐
   │                                             │
   │                                             │
   │                                             │
   │                                             │
   │                                             │
   │                                             │
   └─────────────────────────────────────────────┘

*Critical Thinking*

Would you like to be a farmer? Explain.

_____

_____

_____

# Pat's Farm

Pat has a farm. Her farm has a lot of animals.

The fat, pink pigs are in the pen. The pigs roll in the mud. The pigs eat corn and mash.

The big, brown horses are in the stable. The horses plow the fields. The horses eat apples and carrots.

The short, fluffy chickens are in the coop. Eggs come from chickens. The chickens eat seeds and grit.

The black and white cows are in the pasture. Milk comes from cows. The cows eat grass and grains.

Pat likes being on her farm.

# Prior Knowledge

*Before you read a text, think about what you know about that topic. This will help you understand what you read.*

1. On the chart, write words and phrases that tell what you already know about bats and birds.

bats

both

birds

2. Read the text. Think about how bats and birds are alike. Add words or phrases to the middle of the chart.

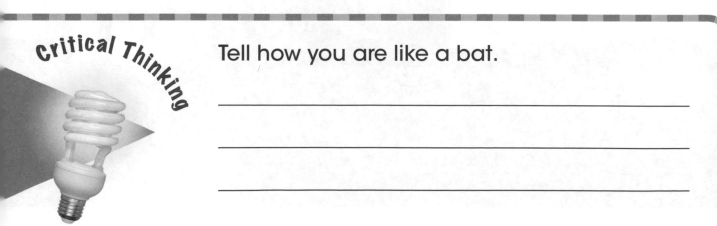

Critical Thinking

Tell how you are like a bat.

_____

_____

_____

# Bats Are Not Birds

Bats are not birds. Bats are mammals. Bats have fur on their bodies. Bats breathe through lungs. Bats are born alive. They drink milk from their mothers. Birds are not mammals. Birds have feathers on their bodies. Birds breathe through air sacs. Birds do not drink milk.

Bats fly at night to look for food. Bats eat fruit, fish, and nectar. Birds fly in the daytime to find food. Birds eat worms, nuts, and seeds. Bats sleep upside down in caves. Birds sleep sitting down in nests.

# Ask Questions

*You may have questions as you read a story. Asking questions helps you learn about the topic. Use who, what, where, when, why, and how.*

1. Read the title. Look at the pictures. Write a question about the title and pictures.

   _____

   _____

2. Read the text. Why does Rosa want to keep the dandelions?

   _____

   _____

3. Rosa protects the plants. What else is Rosa protecting?

   _____

   _____

**Critical Thinking**

What are two things that you can do to protect the planet?

_____

_____

_____

# Protect the Planet

"Dandelions!" Rosa's dad growled. "They're all over the lawn! I'll have to get some spray to get rid of them."

"I think you should leave them," Rosa said. "I like them. Besides, that stuff you put on the lawn is poison. It can hurt people and animals. It pollutes our river, too."

"It does?"

"Sure," Rosa told her dad. "The rain washes that stuff down the drains. The drains empty out into the river. Then the rivers move the water to the ocean. We need to protect the ocean!"

# Ask Questions

*You may have questions as you read a story. Asking questions helps you learn about the topic. Use who, what, where, when, why, and how.*

1. Think about what instruments are in a band. Then read the story.

2. Write a question about each instrument.

Flute: _____

_____

Drums: _____

_____

Guitar: _____

_____

Triangle: _____

_____

**Critical Thinking**

Which instrument would you like to play? Why?

_____

_____

_____

# The School Band

Dev, Mark, Maria, and Ellen are in the school band.

Dev plays the flute. A flute is a tube with holes in it. He blows in a hole at one end of the flute. His fingers cover the holes to make different notes.

Mark plays the drums. He hits the drum with two sticks.

Maria plays the guitar. She strums the strings on the guitar.

Ellen plays the triangle. She hits the triangle with a stick.

Together, Dev, Mark, Maria, and Ellen make beautiful music.

# Ask Questions

**Skill Focus**

*You may have questions as you read a story. Asking questions helps you learn about the topic. Use who, what, where, when, why, and how.*

1. Read the title. Look at the picture. Write a question about the title or picture.

   _____

   _____

2. Read the first three paragraphs. Write a question about what you have read.

   _____

   _____

3. Read the rest of the story. Write a question about it.

   _____

   _____

**Critical Thinking**

Why do you think the kids wanted to surprise their mom?

   _____

   _____

   _____

# The Surprise

Pablo and Bella woke up early. Mom was getting dressed. The kids had to hurry. They wanted to finish before Mom was ready.

The kids crept to the living room. They pulled a box from behind the couch. They took out a roll of wrapping paper.

"She will love this!" said Bella.

Pablo smiled. "This will help her in the garden."

The kids wrapped the gift. Then they heard some noises down the hall. They hopped up and ran toward their mom.

"Surprise!" they shouted.

# Make Connections

*As you read a story, think about how the events are like your own life. This will help you understand what the characters do and how they feel.*

1.  Read the title. What do you know about ice skates?

    _____

    _____

2.  Read the text. Why do you think the Vikings needed ice skates?

    _____

    _____

    _____

**Critical Thinking**

Name one way the Viking skates are like the skates we use today.

_____

_____

_____

# Viking Ice Skates

Have you ever worn ice skates? People have used them for thousands of years. The Vikings made ice skates. These people lived in the north of Europe long, long ago. Vikings are known for being tough and great sailors. But they were skaters, too.

To make a skate, a Viking used a leather shoe. He or she attached a cow's bone to the shoe. The bone was cut and carved so that it worked like a skate blade.

# Make Connections

*As you read a story, think about how the events are like your own life. This will help you understand what the characters do and how they feel.*

1.  Read the title. Look at the pictures. Name one holiday that you celebrate.

    _____

2.  Read the text. Which of the holidays do you celebrate?

    _____

    _____

3.  What kinds of things do you do to celebrate a holiday?

    _____

    _____

**Critical Thinking**

Do all people celebrate holidays in the same way? Explain.

_____

_____

_____

# Holidays

People celebrate holidays.

The Chinese welcome the New Year. They have a parade. They dress up as dragons. They pop firecrackers for good luck. Lanterns light up the streets.

The people in India welcome the New Year, too. They light candles. They wear flowers.

In Mexico, Cinco de Mayo is a holiday. People dance. They eat good food. They have parades, too.

Earth Day is a new holiday. On this day, people take care of the Earth. They plant trees. They clean up trash.

How do you celebrate holidays?

**Earth Day**

**Chinese New Year**

# Make Connections

*As you read a story, think about how the events are like your own life. This will help you understand what the characters do and how they feel.*

1. Read the story. Do you want a free pet? Explain.

   _____

   _____

2. Why did Lisa's mother say she could have a puppy?

   _____

3. Draw a picture of you and a pet. Write a word that tells how you feel about your new pet.

   _____

**Critical Thinking**

Why do you think the people were giving the puppies away?

_____

_____

_____

# Free Puppies

Lisa and her mom were walking home from school.

Lisa saw a sign in a yard that said "Free Puppies."

Lisa asked, "Mom, may I please have a puppy? I will take care of it and will feed it each day."

Mom said, "You have taken care of your fish and kept its jar clean. You play with your baby brother when I am busy. So…yes, you may have a puppy!"

Lisa jumped up and down.

"Yippee!" said Lisa. "Let's go get my puppy!"

# Setting

As you read a story, think about the setting. The setting is where and when the story takes place.

1. Read the story. What made the house "creepy"?

   _____

   _____

2. Draw a picture to show where the story takes place. Write a sentence about the picture.

   ┌─────────────────────────────────────────┐
   │                                         │
   │                                         │
   │                                         │
   │                                         │
   │                                         │
   │                                         │
   └─────────────────────────────────────────┘

   _____

**Critical Thinking**

If you had hit the ball through the window, would you go in to get it? Explain.

_____

_____

_____

# The House

"Let's get out of here," Owen said to Ava. "This place gives me the creeps."

"But we have to get our ball back," Ava said. "It went through that broken window. It must be upstairs." She headed for the big staircase.

Owen followed slowly. He passed a sofa covered with a sheet. He ducked under a cobweb.

"I don't think we should be here," he said.

"Who is going to care? Nobody has lived here for years," said Ava.

# Setting

*As you read a story, think about the setting. The setting is where and when the story takes place.*

1.  Read the title. Look at the pictures. What will you read about?

    _____

    _____

2.  Read the story. Where does the story take place?

    _____

    _____

3.  When does the story take place? How do you know?

    _____

    _____

**Critical Thinking**

How do Marcus and his mom feel when they see Taj marching down the street? Why?

_____

_____

_____

# The Marching Band

Marcus hears the music. "Listen!" he cries. "I hear it!" Marcus and his mom look down the street. They see the band marching toward them.

Marcus sees the flutes. "Taj should be coming by soon," he told his mom. The flutes passed. Marcus shouts, "There he is, Mom!" Marcus waves to his brother.

Soon the parade is over. Marcus and his mom wait for Taj to meet them. "You were great," Marcus told Taj.

"Thanks," Taj said. "It was fun, but I am tired. Let's go home."

# Setting

*As you read a story, think about the setting. The setting is where and when the story takes place.*

1. Read the story. Where does the story take place?

   _____

2. Draw a picture to show where the story takes place. Write a sentence about the picture.

   _____

   _____

**Critical Thinking**

Why do you think the other ship wanted to sneak by Grick and Gleep?

_____

_____

_____

# The Spaceship

"I don't get it," Gleep said. He stared at the control panel. Then he looked out the window. All he could see was the black of deep space and some stars. "The screen shows us heading for another ship. But nothing is out there."

Grick floated to Gleep's side. He studied the screen with his five eyes. "The other ship must have a shield up," he said. "The driver must want to sneak past us."

# Plot

*A story has a plot. The plot is the story's action. The action tells what happens.*

1. Read the title. Write one thing that you already know about the topic.

   _____

   _____

2. Read the story. What happens first in the story?

   _____

   _____

3. What made you want to keep on reading the story?

   _____

   _____

   _____

**Critical Thinking**

If a genie had been inside the bottle, what do you think the boys would have done?

_____

_____

_____

# Genie in a Bottle

Lee and Todd found a bottle. The bottle looked old.

"Maybe it's a magic bottle!" said Lee.

"Maybe there's a genie inside!" said Todd.

"Let's rub it," said Lee. They rubbed it. Nothing happened.

"Let's turn it over. Maybe a genie will fall out," said Todd. They turned it over. Nothing happened.

"Rats!" said Lee.

"Let's take the bottle home to Mom," said Todd.

They picked flowers to put in the bottle. They didn't find a magic bottle, but Mom would have a new vase!

# Plot

*A story has a plot. The plot is the story's action. The action tells what happens.*

1. Read the first paragraph of the story. What is the problem?

   _____

2. What do the girls plan to do to solve the problem?

   _____

3. Read the second paragraph. What is the new problem?

   _____

4. Draw a picture to show how the new problem is solved.

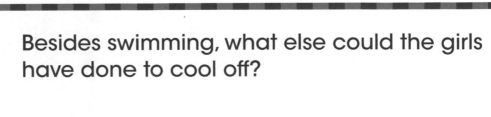

Critical Thinking

Besides swimming, what else could the girls have done to cool off?

   _____

   _____

   _____

# Buzzing Bees

The two girls went out into the backyard. It was a hot day. The pool looked cool and refreshing. The girls were ready to go for a swim.

There was a swarm of buzzing bees. The girls ducked their heads and ran around the picnic table on the grass. The bees still buzzed around. Finally, the girls ran inside the house.

The girls heard a swishing sound. The sprinklers came on. The bees flew away. Finally, the girls could jump into the cool pool!

# Plot

*A story has a plot. The plot is the story's action. The action tells what happens.*

1. Read the title. Read the story. Who are the characters in the story?

   _____     _____

2. What do Manny and Jack do together after school?

   _____

   _____

3. Now that Manny knows where Jack lives, where do you think the boys will play? Why?

   _____

   _____

   _____

**Critical Thinking**

What can you tell about Manny by the way he treats his friend?

_____

_____

_____

# The New Kid

Manny liked the new kid, Jack. Manny asked Jack to come over after school. The two boys had a great time.

Manny wanted to go to Jack's house next. But Jack never asked him. Manny felt hurt and angry.

Then Manny saw where Jack lived. The building was rundown and in a bad part of town. Manny thought Jack might feel bad about where he lived. He guessed that was why Jack hadn't asked him over. Manny didn't feel angry anymore.

# Characters

The characters are the people in a story. You can tell what the characters are like by what they say, what they do, and how they treat others.

1. Read the title of the story. Think about when and why people say "thank you."

2. Read the story. How does Jo feel about helping her mom?

_____

_____

3. How does Jo feel about helping her dad and Mrs. Jones?

_____

_____

_____

**Critical Thinking**

Do you like to help people? Why?

_____

_____

_____

# Thank You, Jo!

Jo lives in an apartment with her mom and dad. Jo likes to help people.

Jo feels happy when she helps her mom. She takes out the trash for her mom. Her mom says, "Thank you, Jo!"

Jo helps her dad wash the car. They have fun together. Her dad says, "Thank you, Jo!"

Jo also helps Mrs. Jones. Mrs. Jones lives alone next door. Jo picks up the mail for Mrs. Jones. Mrs. Jones gives Jo a big hug and says, "Thank you, Jo!"

CORBIS

# Characters

The characters are the people in a story. You can tell what the characters are like by what they say, what they do, and how they treat others.

1. Read the title. Have you ever had an invisible friend? What was your invisible friend like?

   _____

   _____

2. Read the story. Does Adam tell his mother the truth? Explain.

   _____

   _____

3. Why does Adam blame Skip?

   _____

   _____

**Critical Thinking**

Would you like to have a friend like Adam? Explain.

_____

_____

_____

# The Invisible Friend

My friend, Skip, is invisible.

"Adam! Get in here now!"

"Yes, Mother?" I said.

"Did you color on the wall?" asked Mom.

"No, Mother. Skip did," I said. "This is my friend, Skip."

"There is no one there!" said Mom.

"You can't see him, Mom. He is invisible," I said.

"Well, you and your invisible friend are in trouble for coloring on the walls."

"Ahhh, Mom! Can't you just punish Skip?" I asked.

"Nope. He's your friend. You help him clean the wall," Mom said.

# Characters

*The characters are the people in a story. You can tell what the characters are like by what they say, what they do, and how they treat others.*

1. Read the title. Look at the pictures. What will you read about?

   _____

   _____

2. Read the story. Write two words that tell about Tracy.

   _____     _____

3. Write two things that Tracy will do on her trip.

   _____

   _____

   _____

**Critical Thinking**

Pretend that Tracy is going to camp on her trip. What else should she pack?

   _____

   _____

   _____

# Tracy's Trip

It was the night before Tracy's trip with her parents. Tracy could not wait. They were going to the mountains.

She packed for the trip. She packed warm clothes. She packed her camera, too. She wanted to take pictures. She packed her bird book. She hoped to see some birds.

Tracy was almost ready. Then she remembered her journal! She wanted to write about each day of her trip.

Tracy lay on her bed. She was thinking of her trip. Soon, she drifted off to sleep.

# Title and Headings

*Before reading a text, read the title and headings. The title and headings will tell you what you will read about.*

1. Read the title. Read each heading. What will you read about?

   _____

   _____

2. Read the text. Write one fact about each heading.

   A Tall Home: _____

   _____

   A Painted Home: _____

   _____

   A Dry Home: _____

   _____

Critical Thinking

Pretend that you will design a new kind of house. What would it look like?

   _____

   _____

   _____

# Homes

People live in different kinds of homes.

### A Tall Home

This home is in an apartment building. There are many homes inside. Many families live here.

### A Painted Home

This home is painted in bright colors. It has a green door and red walls inside. Some homes are only one color. This one is many colors.

### A Dry Home

These homes are in a warm, rainy place. Each roof is made of leaves. Rain slides off the leaves and drops to the ground.

# Title and Headings

*Skill Focus*

*Before reading a text, read the title and headings. The title and headings will tell you what you will read about.*

1. Read the title. Read the headings. What will you read about?

   _____

2. Read the text. Write a fact about each heading.

   Shapes in Paintings: _____

   _____

   Shapes in Sculptures: _____

   _____

   Shapes in Windows: _____

   _____

*Critical Thinking*

Use your favorite shapes to make a picture.

```



```

# SHAPES IN ART

You can see shapes in art. Think about paintings and sculptures. What kinds of shapes can you see?

## Shapes in Paintings

An artist makes a painting. Some paintings have many shapes. You may see squares, rectangles, circles, and ovals. The shapes make a design. The shapes may tell a story, too.

## Shapes in Sculptures

A sculpture is made of wood or stone. Sculptures use many shapes, too.

## Shapes in Windows

Stained glass windows are pretty. The windows have shapes and patterns.

**This painting has many shapes. Can you see squares and rectangles?**

# Title and Headings

*Before reading a text, read the title and headings. The title and headings will tell you what you will read about.*

1. Read the title. Read the headings. What will you read about?

   _____

2. Read the text. Write a fact about each heading.

   Food: _____

   _____

   Exercise: _____

   _____

   Sleep: _____

   _____

## Critical Thinking

Draw a picture of what you do to stay healthy.

# Staying Healthy

You are growing fast. You need to take care of yourself.

**Food**

The right foods help you grow strong. Fruits and vegetables are good.

**Exercise**

Exercise will make you strong and healthy. Run every day. Playing sports is a good way to run and have some fun.

**Sleep**

Get a good sleep every night. When you sleep well, you will be ready for the next day.

Take good care of yourself. You will be glad you did.

**Eat healthy snacks.**

**Exercise every day.**

**Get enough sleep.**

# Typeface and Captions

*Typeface (style of letters) helps you see important facts. Captions tell about pictures or charts. The typeface and captions can help you understand what you read.*

1. Read the title. Look at the pictures.

2. Read the captions. What did you learn by reading the captions and looking at each picture?

_____

_____

_____

3. Read the text. Which words are boldface? Why are these words boldface?

_____

_____

## Critical Thinking

How do rules keep us safe?

_____

_____

_____

# Rules for Crossing the Street

Use crosswalks.

Do you like to take walks? What do you do when you want to cross the street? You need to be safe. Here are good rules for crossing streets.

1. **Do not** cross in the middle of the street.

2. Always cross at the corner crosswalks.

3. At lights, look for the "walk" sign. Cross when the sign says "walk."

4. Even at lights, always look both ways first.

5. Cross the street quickly. But be safe, too.

Look for the "walk" sign.

Look both ways.

# Typeface and Captions

*Typeface (style of letters) helps you see important facts. Captions tell about pictures or charts. The typeface and captions can help you understand what you read.*

1. Read the title. Look at the picture. Read the caption. What will you read about?

   _____

   _____

2. Read the text. Draw a sea animal from the text. Add a caption to the picture.

   _____

   _____

   _____

**Critical Thinking**

How are sea animals alike? How are they different?

_____

_____

_____

# SEA LIFE

Many animals and plants live in the sea.

Sea horses live in shallow water.

Sea stars and sea urchins live in tide pools. They are both small creatures. They come and go with the tides.

Whales can dive deep. But they are mammals. Mammals have to come up for air.

Sharks are a kind of fish. They do not need to come up for air. They have gills to breathe. They swim all the time. They are always looking for fish to eat.

**A seahorse, sea star, and shark live in the sea.**

# Typeface and Captions

Typeface (style of letters) helps you see important facts. Captions tell about pictures or charts. The typeface and captions can help you understand what you read.

1. Look at the picture. Read the caption. What do you think you will read about?

   _____

   _____

2. Read the text. Draw a picture of the type of shoe that you would like to wear.

Critical Thinking

Design a new kind of shoe. Describe it.

   _____

   _____

   _____

# SUPER SHOES

When is a shoe not just a shoe? When it's also a roller skate or a compass! Here are some crazy shoe styles kids have worn.

## Compass Shoes

A compass tells you which way you are going. Compass shoes have a compass in the heel. These shoes can keep you from getting lost.

## Skate Shoes

These shoes have hidden wheels in the bottom. They change into skates! Then you can go fast.

## Light-up Shoes

These shoes light up whenever you move.

**Skate shoes have wheels.**

# Graphics

*Pictures, drawings, and charts are graphics. Graphics help you understand and remember what you have read.*

1. Read the text. Look at the graphics. Write two words or phrases to describe each graphic in this text.

   Desert: _____ _____

   Prairie: _____ _____

   Rainforest: _____ _____

2. Draw a picture to go with the text below.

   See the beach. It is sandy.

   ┌─────────────────────────────────────────┐
   │                                         │
   │                                         │
   │                                         │
   │                                         │
   │                                         │
   │                                         │
   └─────────────────────────────────────────┘

*Critical Thinking*

If you could live anywhere, where would you live? Explain.

_____

_____

_____

# LAND

desert

There are many kinds of land.

## Desert

The desert is hot and dry. The soil is sandy. There are not many plants and animals here.

## Prairie

prairie

The prairie has a lot of grass. It is hot in the summer and cold in the winter. Many animals live here.

## Rainforest

rainforest

The rainforest is full of trees. The rainforest is not too hot or too cold. It gets a lot of rain each year. Many plants and animals live here.

# Graphics

Pictures, drawings, and charts are graphics. Graphics help you understand and remember what you have read.

1.  Read the title. Look at the pictures. What will you read about?

    _____

2.  Read the text. Write one way that people have changed space.

    _____

    _____

3.  Draw your favorite space machine.

Critical Thinking

Why do people want to learn about space?

    _____

    _____

    _____

# People and Outer Space

People have changed space. We send things into space.

We send satellites into space. They fly around Earth. They take pictures of Earth.

We send space stations into orbit. People can live there. They can learn about space.

We fly rockets to the moon. There, we can learn more about the moon.

We send probes far into space. The probes take pictures of things in space. The pictures show what space looks like.

Spitzer Space Telescope

space shuttle

# Graphics

*Pictures, drawings, and charts are graphics. Graphics help you understand and remember what you have read.*

1. Read the title. Look at the pictures. What do the pictures show?

   _____

2. Read the text. List the stages of a frog's life.

   _____

   _____

3. Draw one part of a frog's life. Write a sentence about your drawing.

   _____

**Critical Thinking**

What would happen to the frog if it stayed as a tadpole?

_____

_____

_____

# A Frog's Life

A mother frog lives in a pond. She is ready to lay eggs. She lays eggs in the water. Each egg can become a frog.

When the eggs hatch, tadpoles come out. A tadpole looks like a little fish.

The tadpole grows. It looks like a fish with two legs!

Then it grows two more legs. Now it has four legs. It looks more like a frog. Now it is called a froglet.

Each young frog becomes an adult frog. Then the cycle starts again.

frog eggs

tadpoles

adult frog

froglet

#50724—Read and Succeed: Comprehension Level 1

# Main Idea

The main idea of a paragraph tells what all of its sentences are about. As you read a paragraph, ask, "What are the sentences telling me?"

1. Read the story. Then reread the first paragraph. Write the main idea.

   _____

2. How did Detective Joe help find the lost bike? Write three details below.

   _____

   _____

   _____

3. Reread the last paragraph. Write the main idea.

   _____

**Critical Thinking**

Think about a time you lost something. What did you do to find the lost item?

_____

_____

# Detective Joe

There was a kid detective named Detective Joe. He liked to solve mysteries. Detective Joe saw a boy crying. The boy had lost his bike.

Joe told the boy not to worry because he would help. He asked the boy questions. He wrote down what the boy said.

Joe used his magnifying glass to look for clues. He went up and down the street. He found the missing bike. The boy had left it at a friend's house. Joe had solved another mystery!

# Main Idea

The main idea of a paragraph tells what all of its sentences are about. As you read a paragraph, ask, "What are the sentences telling me?"

1. Read the text. Draw a picture that shows what the text is about.

2. Write the main idea for the following paragraphs.

Paragraph 1: _____

Paragraph 2: _____

Paragraph 3: _____

Critical Thinking

What kind of weather do you like best? Why?

_____

_____

_____

# THE WEATHER

The weather is all around us. The sun can shine. That is weather. The wind can blow. That is weather. The rain can fall. That is weather.

Sometimes the weather is good. It is a pretty day. It is a day to go outside and play.

Sometimes the weather is bad. It is windy. The wind is blowing very hard. It is not a good day to go out and play.

The weather may be good or bad. You will have to wait and see!

sunny weather

rainy weather

# Main Idea

*The main idea of a paragraph tells what all of its sentences are about. As you read a paragraph, ask, "What are the sentences telling me?"*

1. Read the title. Look at the pictures. What will you read about?

   _____

2. Read the text. Draw a picture to show the main idea of the text. Write a sentence about the picture.

   ```
   ┌─────────────────────────────────────────────┐
   │                                             │
   │                                             │
   │                                             │
   │                                             │
   │                                             │
   │                                             │
   │                                             │
   └─────────────────────────────────────────────┘
   ```

   _____

**Critical Thinking**

What might happen if the bike did not unfold?

_____

_____

_____

# A New Kind of Bike

Can you store your bike in your closet?  Can you take it on a bus?  You could if you had a folding bike. These new bikes can go places where other bikes can't go.

Folding bikes are great if you live high up in a tall building. These bikes fit on an elevator.

Folding bikes can come along on subways and trains, too. You could pack one to take to your grandma's house!

# Details

*The main idea is what the paragraph or story is about. The details tell about the main idea.*

1. Read the story. Look for the main idea and details that tell about it.

2. Write details that tell about the main idea below.

Main Idea: Ben likes to do magic.

Detail: _____

_____

_____

Detail: _____

_____

_____

## Critical Thinking

Invent a new magic trick. How does the trick work?

_____

_____

_____

# Ben's Magic Tricks

Ben likes to do magic. He has a tall black magic hat. Ben has a long magic wand, too.

With the black hat and magic wand, Ben can do many tricks. Ben taps the hat with the wand. He pulls a rabbit from the hat. Ben taps the hat again. A card comes out of the hat. Ben can do more magic tricks. He taps the hat two times. This time, a flower comes out of the hat.

Ben loves his magic hat and wand!

# Details

*The main idea is what the paragraph or story is about. The details tell about the main idea.*

1. Read the text. Look for the main idea. Look for the details that tell about the main idea.

2. Write details that tell about the main idea of the second paragraph.

   Main Idea: In the forest, there are plants.

   Detail: _____

   _____

   Detail: _____

   _____

   Detail: _____

   _____

Critical Thinking

What would happen if there weren't any forests?

_____

_____

_____

# The Living Forest

The forest is home to many living things.

In the forest, there are plants. There are big trees. There are small flowers. There are green grasses.

In the forest, there are lots of animals. There are big animals. There are animals that fly. There are animals that climb trees.

In the forest, there is water. There are rivers with fish. There are ponds with frogs. There are waterfalls.

The forest is alive with lots of living things.

# Details

*The main idea is what the paragraph or story is about. The details tell about the main idea.*

1. Read the text. Look for the main idea. Look for the details.

2. Write three details that tell about the main idea below.

   Main Idea: Robert collects rocks.

   Detail: _____

   _____

   Detail: _____

   _____

   Detail: _____

   _____

**Critical Thinking**

What do you collect? Why?

_____

_____

_____

# Robert's Collection

Robert collects rocks. He collects big rocks and small rocks. He collects brown rocks and green rocks. He collects bumpy rocks and smooth rocks.

Robert keeps his rocks in a big jar. Robert can see in the jar. He likes to look at all the rocks he has collected.

Robert takes the rocks out of the jar and puts them on his bed. Robert counts the rocks. He sorts the rocks by color, by shape, and by size. Robert puts the rocks back in the jar.

# Main Idea and Details

*The main idea is what the story is about. The details are the facts that tell about the main idea.*

1. Read the text. What is this text about?

   _____

2. Write three details that tell about the main idea below.

   Main Idea: Volcanoes have a good side.

   Detail: _____

   _____

   Detail: _____

   _____

   Detail: _____

   _____

**Critical Thinking**

How can volcanoes hurt people?

_____

_____

_____

# NOT ALL BAD

Volcanoes are deadly. But did you know they have a good side, too? Read on to find out what it is.

When a volcano erupts, it shoots ash into the air. The ash falls to the ground. The ash is good for the soil. It makes plants grow fast.

When a volcano erupts, lava comes out the top. Silver and gold are found in places where lava once was.

When a volcano erupts, it is very hot. Some people heat homes or water with the heat from volcanoes.

# Main Idea and Details

*The main idea is what the story is about. The details are the facts that tell about the main idea.*

1. Read the text. What is it mostly about?

   _____

2. Write three details that tell about the main idea below.

   Main Idea: Gravity is a force.

   Detail: _____

   _____

   Detail: _____

   _____

   Detail: _____

   _____

**Critical Thinking**

What would life be like without gravity?

_____

_____

_____

# Gravity

Gravity is a force. It is very strong. You cannot see it. You cannot touch it. It makes the planets go around the sun. It keeps the moon going around Earth.

Gravity makes things fall to the ground. It holds us on the ground, too. Without gravity, we would float into space. This would make life pretty hard!

**Gravity pulls this girl down the hill.**

# Time Order

*Most stories are told in time order. This is the order in which things happen—from first to last.*

1.  Read the story. Think about what happens first, second, third, next, and last in the story.

2.  Number the sentences in the correct order from 1–5.

    _____ The baby turtle comes out of the egg.

    _____ The egg sits in the mud.

    _____ A leg comes out of the egg.

    _____ The egg begins to crack.

    _____ The baby turtle swims away.

3.  Make a list of other animals that hatch from eggs.

    _____

    _____

**Critical Thinking**

Why do you think the baby turtle is able to swim right after being born?

_____

_____

_____

# Down by the Pond

Anna and Levi saw a big egg in the mud. It was cracking.

"What kind of egg is it?" asked Anna.

"I don't know," said Levi.

A leg came out of the egg.

Then a head came out of the egg.

A baby turtle came out of the egg. The turtle had a green shell. It had a head, four legs, and a little tail. It looked just like its mom and dad.

The turtle slowly walked to the water, dove in, and swam away.

# Time Order

*Most stories are told in time order. This is the order in which things happen—from first to last.*

1. Read the story. Think about what the girls did at recess.

2. Read the sentences. Number the sentences in the correct order from 1–6.

_____ The girls play on the jungle gym.

_____ Recess is over.

_____ The girls jump rope.

_____ The girls walk to the playground.

_____ The girls swing on the swings.

_____ The girls walk back to class.

## Critical Thinking

What could happen next in the story?

_____

_____

_____

# Recess Fun

It's time for morning recess!  Jan and Bree walk to the playground. They play together at recess.

First, the girls jump rope.  Jan jumps 10 times in a row.  Bree jumps 12 times in a row!

Next, the girls run to the swings.  Jan swings up high.  Bree swings fast.

Finally, the girls race to the jungle gym. They climb up to the top. They hang from the ropes and giggle.

Recess is over.  Jan and Bree walk back to class.

# Time Order

*Most stories are told in time order. This is the order in which things happen—from first to last.*

1. Read the text. What is the text about?

   _____

2. Number the sentences in the correct order from 1–4.

   _____ Today, planes are big and fast.

   _____ Orville flew the plane in 1903.

   _____ In 1927, Charles Lindbergh flew over the ocean.

   _____ In 1853, the first glider was flown.

3. Draw a picture of an airplane from long ago.

**Critical Thinking**

How are planes today different from planes long ago?

_____

_____

_____

# History of Planes

1903

1927

Today

People have always dreamed of flying.

In 1853, the first glider was flown. It was like a plane. It used the wind to fly.

The Wright brothers built the first plane. Orville flew the plane in 1903. He did not fly far or high. But he did fly!

In 1927, Charles Lindbergh flew over the ocean. He flew from New York to France. It took 33 hours.

Today, planes are big and fast. People fly all over the world.

# Logical Order

*Logical order tells the steps for doing a task. The steps are in an order that makes sense. This helps the reader understand and follow them.*

1. Read the title. Read the story.

2. Read the sentences. Number the sentences in the correct order from 1–6.

_____ He got used to singing in public.

_____ Luis joined his school's choir and band.

_____ The judges chose him for the show.

_____ Luis was too scared to try out for the TV talent show.

_____ He sang at choir and band practice.

_____ Luis tried out for the TV talent show.

**Critical Thinking**

Even though Luis was nervous, why do you think he wanted to try out for the show?

_____

_____

_____

# Luis Gets Ready

Luis's friends wanted him to try out for a TV talent show. Luis was too scared to try out. He had never sung in front of a crowd. He thought he needed practice.

Luis joined his school's choir and a band. He sang at choir practice. He sang at band practice, too. He got used to singing in public. Soon, he felt ready to try out for the talent show.

On his tryout day, Luis sang well. The judges chose him for the show!

# Logical Order

**Skill Focus**

*Logical order tells the steps for doing a task. The steps are in an order that makes sense. This helps the reader understand and follow them.*

1.  Read the text. Which words help you know which order to complete each part of the task?

    _____  _____  _____

    _____  _____

2.  Read the sentences. Number the sentences in the correct order from 1–4.

    _____ Leaves begin to grow.

    _____ The plant grows above the ground.

    _____ There is a seed.

    _____ The roots grow down into the soil.

**Critical Thinking**

Write the steps for brushing your teeth in logical order. Then act out each step.

_____

_____

_____

# How Plants Grow

Do you know how plants grow? First, there is a seed. It is under the ground. Next, roots grow down into the soil. The roots get food and water for the plant. Then, leaves begin to grow. The leaves grow up.

Soon, the plant will be above the ground. Then, there is a plant growing in the sun. We can watch it grow tall.

**Roots in the soil get food and water for the plant.**

# Logical Order

*Logical order tells the steps for doing a task. The steps are in an order that makes sense. This helps the reader understand and follow them.*

1. Read the title. What do you think you will learn?

   _____

   _____

2. Read the text. Then read the sentences. Number the sentences in the correct order from 1–5.

   _____ Shift your feet to the top of the board.

   _____ Push the tail down.

   _____ Land with your knees still bent.

   _____ Put one foot in the middle of the board.

   _____ Pull your knees to your chest.

## Critical Thinking

Invent a trick you can do on a skateboard or bike or with a jump rope. Tell about it.

_____

_____

_____

# A Skateboard Trick

An *ollie* is a skateboard jump. Here's how to do one.

First, put one foot in the middle of the board. Put the other on the board's tail.

Then, push the tail down so it smacks the ground and the board flies up.

As the board flies, pull your knees to your chest. Shift your feet to the top of the board.

Finally, land with your knees still bent.

Now, put on your helmet and kneepads and get out there and try an ollie!

# Retell

*When you retell a story, you use your own words.*

1.  Read the text. Then use your own words to retell it.

    Tigers are _____ .

    Tigers like to _____ .

    A tiger's stripes help it _____ .

    At night, tigers _____ .

2.  Draw a picture of a tiger.

    ┌─────────────────────────────────────────┐
    │                                         │
    │                                         │
    │                                         │
    │                                         │
    │                                         │
    └─────────────────────────────────────────┘

**Critical Thinking**

How is a tiger like a pet cat?

_____

_____

_____

# Big Cats in the Wild

A tiger is a big, strong cat. A tiger lives in the wild.

Tigers love water. They are good swimmers. When a tiger is hot, it will jump into the water.

A tiger has a coat of fur. The tiger's coat has stripes on it. The stripes help the tiger hide from other animals. The tiger hides in the grass or by trees when it is hunting for food.

A tiger hunts at night. A tiger hunts big animals like deer and wild pigs.

# Retell

*When you retell a story, you use your own words.*

1. Read the title. Read the text.

2. Retell the text using your own words.

   A man in England bought a _____

   _____ .

   He used it to _____

   _____ .

   He found _____

   _____ .

   Experts came _____

   _____ .

**Critical Thinking**

What can we learn from the treasures the man found?

_____

_____

_____

# Digging Up the Past

Have you ever used a metal detector? This tool is used to find metal in the ground, like coins or gold. But one man in England found lots of cool things! He was hunting for metal on a farm. He dug up gold sword handles. He found silver crosses. He found many things from long ago! Experts came to see it all. They said it was a king's treasure. The king had lived long ago. The metal detector helped the man "dig up the past."

# Retell

*When you retell a story, you use your own words.*

1. Read the story. Then use your own words to retell it.

_____

_____

_____

_____

2. Draw a picture to go with your retelling.

```
┌─────────────────────────────────────┐
│                                     │
│                                     │
│                                     │
│                                     │
│                                     │
└─────────────────────────────────────┘
```

**Critical Thinking**

What would happen if a dog came to live at the house?

_____

_____

_____

# Strange Friends

Cat and Mouse live in a house. Cat has a big bed. Mouse has a small bed.

Cat and Mouse are friends. Cat is big. Mouse is small.

Cat and Mouse eat people food. Cat drinks milk. Mouse eats cheese.

Cat and Mouse chase things. Cat chases a ball. Mouse chases string.

Cat and Mouse like to nap. Cat naps in the window. Mouse naps on the floor.

Cat and Mouse are two strange friends. They will be friends forever.

# Cause and Effect

*The cause tells why something happened. The effect tells what happened.*

1. Read the text. Then write the effect for each cause.

| Cause | Effect |
|---|---|
| The crust is made of big pieces of land. | |
| The mantle is a thick and hot layer of rock. | |
| Magma comes out of a volcano. | |

**Critical Thinking**

Pretend that you forgot to set your alarm clock. What might be the effect?

_____

_____

_____

# EARTH'S LAYERS

The earth is made of layers. The outside layer is the *crust*. The crust is made of big pieces of land. The pieces of land push against each other.

Under the crust is the *mantle*. It is a thick and hot layer of rock. This rock can melt. The melted rock is called *magma*.

Magma comes out of a volcano. Then it is called *lava*. Lava can be fast and runny. Or, it can be slow and thick. Either way, lava is very hot!

# Cause and Effect

The cause tells why something happened. The effect tells what happened.

1. Read the story. Then write the effect for each cause.

| Cause | Effect |
|---|---|
| Marty's family ran out of milk. | |
| Dad left the keys in the house. | |
| Dad locked his keys in the house. | |
| The window was open. | |

**Critical Thinking**

What might have happened if the window had not been open?

_____

_____

_____

# A Trip to the Store

"We're out of milk," said Dad.

"Let's go to the store," said Marty.

They got into the car. Dad couldn't start the car. "I left my keys in the house," said Dad.

They went back to the house. The door wouldn't open. "I locked the door," said Dad. "Now we can't get into the house."

"The kitchen window is open," said Marty.

Marty climbed through the window. He found the keys and opened the front door.

Dad and Marty were on their way to the store.

# Compare and Contrast

You can compare two items. This means you find something that is similar or the same about both of them. You can contrast two items, too. This means you find something that is different about them.

1.  Read the story. What is the same about a city and a ranch?

    _____

2.  Complete the chart about a city and a ranch.

|  | City | Ranch |
|---|---|---|
| See |  |  |
| Do |  |  |
| Sleep |  |  |

**Critical Thinking**

Would you like to go to a city or a ranch? Explain.

_____

_____

_____

# The Family Vacation

Ken and his family were going on a trip. They could go to a big city or to a ranch.

In the city, he could see a play. But at a ranch, he could see the hills.

In the city, he could ride on the subway. But at a ranch, he could ride on a horse.

In the city, he could sleep in a hotel. But at a ranch, he could sleep by a campfire.

Where should Ken and his family go on their trip?

# Compare and Contrast

You can compare two items. This means you find something that is similar or the same about both of them. You can contrast two items, too. This means you find something that is different about them.

1.  Read the text. Then write words or phrases on the chart to compare and contrast ladybugs and bees.

ladybugs

_____

_____

_____

_____

_____

both

_____

_____

_____

_____

_____

bees

_____

_____

_____

_____

_____

**Critical Thinking**

Which bug do you think is the most helpful? Explain.

_____

_____

_____

# Helpful Bugs

Ladybugs and bees are bugs. They are helpful bugs.

Ladybugs eat aphids. Aphids are bad bugs. They eat the leaves and stems on plants. Ladybugs eat the aphids. Ladybugs keep the plants healthy and strong.

Bees sip the nectar from flowers. The bees use the nectar to make honey. People like to eat honey.

What other bugs are helpful?

# Author's Purpose

*Authors write stories for many reasons: to inform, to entertain, to persuade, or to make readers feel a certain way.*

1. Read the text. What is the author writing about?

   _____

2. Why did the author write this text?

   _____

   _____

3. Did the story change how you feel about apples? Why or why not?

   _____

   _____

   _____

**Critical Thinking**

Do you agree that apples are better than oranges? Explain.

_____

_____

_____

# Apples Are Better Than Oranges

There are red, yellow, and green apples. Oranges are just orange.

Apples are a great snack. Just wash the apple and eat! You have to wash and peel an orange. Then you can eat it.

Apples are used to make many foods. Apples are used to make juice, cakes, and pies. Oranges are mostly used to make orange juice.

That is why apples are better than oranges.

# Author's Purpose

*Authors write stories for many reasons: to inform, to entertain, to persuade, or to make readers feel a certain way.*

1.  Read the text. Write three things that you learned.

    _____

    _____

    _____

2.  Why do you think the author wrote this text?

    _____

    _____

3.  When do you use a clock or calendar?

    _____

    _____

Critical Thinking

In 100 years, what might people use to keep track of time?

_____

_____

_____

# Measuring Time

We cannot see or touch time. Time is when things happen.

Measuring time is important. Clocks help you get to school on time. Calendars help you know when it is your birthday.

In the past, people did not have clocks or calendars. People used the sun and moon to tell time. They used the stars and planets, too.

Today, we use clocks to tell time. We use calendars to know when things will happen. These things help us keep track of time.

# Table of Contents

**Skill Focus**

*Nonfiction (or true) books have a table of contents. The table of contents shows the important topics (or chapters) covered in the book.*

1. Read the table of contents. What is this book about?

   _____

2. How can a table of contents help you find information?

   _____

   _____

3. What other information is in the table of contents?

   _____

   _____

**Critical Thinking**

What is another topic or chapter title that would fit this book?

_____

_____

_____

# A Visit to a Farm

## Table of Contents

# Table of Contents

*Nonfiction (or true) books have a table of contents. The table of contents shows the important topics (or chapters) covered in the book.*

1. Read the table of contents. What other topic, or chapter, would you add to the table of contents?

   _____

2. Draw a picture of what the "Horses at Work" chapter might be about. Write a sentence about the picture.

   +-------------------------------------------------+
   |                                                 |
   |                                                 |
   |                                                 |
   |                                                 |
   |                                                 |
   +-------------------------------------------------+

   _____

**Critical Thinking**

What is another animal that you would like to read about? Explain.

_____

_____

_____

# Horses

## Table of Contents

# Index

Many nonfiction books have an index. The index is in the back of a book. The index tells you where you can read about different topics.

1. Read the index. What is this book about?

   _____

   _____

2. How are the items listed in the index?

   _____

   _____

3. On what pages could you read about sirens?

   _____

**Critical Thinking**

How can an index help you?

_____

_____

_____

# Firefighters

## Index

# Index

**Skill Focus**

Many nonfiction books have an index. The index is in the back of a book. The index tells you where you can read about different topics.

1. Read the index. What countries are listed in the index?

   _____

   _____

2. Name three kinds of food that you could read about in "Breakfast Around the World."

   _____

   _____

3. On what pages could you read about fruits?

   _____

**Critical Thinking**

Pretend that you will make an index. What kinds of things would you include?

_____

_____

_____

# Breakfast Around the World

## Index

# Glossary

**Skill Focus**

*Some books have a glossary. A glossary is like a dictionary. It gives information about words in that book.*

1. Read the glossary. What information is given in the glossary?

   _____

   _____

2. Would the words in this glossary belong in a book about Japan? Why or why not?

   _____

   _____

   _____

**Critical Thinking**

How is a glossary different from an index?

_____

_____

_____

# Canada

## Glossary

**Canada**—a large country in North America

**caribou**—a type of deer

**evergreen**—a plant that stays green all year

**forests**—land that has many trees

**hockey**—a sport played on ice with sticks and a puck

**meadows**—land that is covered with grass

**narwhal**—a type of whale that lives in arctic waters

**North America**—one of the seven continents in the world

**plains**—open areas of land

**prairie**—a wide area of grassland

**shores**—land along the edges of bodies of water

# Glossary

Some books have a glossary. A glossary is like a dictionary. It gives information about words in that book.

1. Read the glossary. Pick a word. Write the word and its meaning.

   _____

   _____

2. Why do you think these words are listed in the glossary?

   _____

   _____

   _____

**Critical Thinking**

How are a glossary and a dictionary alike?

_____

_____

_____

# Earthquakes

## Glossary

**crust**—top layer of the earth

**diagram**—drawing that shows how something works

**earthquake**—shaking of the earth caused by plate movement and the release of pressure

**focus**—center of an earthquake

**plate**—section of the earth's crust

**pressure**—great force

## Answer Key

**Preview, p. 8**

1. Answers will vary. Sample: I will read about a boy who has some kittens.

2. Answers will vary. Sample: Cats are mammals; Cats are furry; Cats are pets.

3. Answers will vary. Sample: The kittens were born in the morning; The kittens still had their eyes closed.

Critical Thinking answers will vary. Sample: It lets me know what I will read about.

**Preview, p. 10**

1. Answers will vary. Sample: I will read about horses.

2. Answers will vary. Sample: Horses are big. Horses live on farms. Horses eat hay.

3. Answers will vary. Sample: Horses live all over the world. Some horses are wild.

Critical Thinking answers will vary. Sample: Wild horses live on plains. Pet horses live in stables.

**Preview, p. 12**

1. Answers will vary. Sample: I will read about maps.

2. Answers will vary. Sample: It will give me an idea about what I will read.

3. Answers will vary. Sample: Maps can be drawn to show different places.

Critical Thinking answers will vary. Sample: People would have to stop and ask for directions. People would get lost a lot.

**Predict, p. 14**

1. Answers will vary. Sample: A boy might lose a tooth.

2. Answers will vary. Sample: He wiggled the loose tooth with his tongue.

3. Answers will vary. Sample: I think he will put it under his pillow so the tooth fairy will come.

Critical Thinking answers will vary. Sample: No, applesauce is not hard enough to pull out a tooth.

## Answer Key (cont.)

### Predict, p. 16

1. Answers will vary. Sample: A wish is something that you hope will come true.
2. Answers will vary. Sample: I think that Liz will wish to be a princess.
3. Answers will vary. Sample: Yes, I wished for a puppy and I got one for my birthday.

Critical Thinking answers will vary. Sample: I would wish for new shoes, a kitten, and to be a basketball player when I grow up.

### Predict, p. 18

1. Answers will vary. Sample: Sir Robert had been travelling for a long time.
2. Drawings and answers will vary. Sample: I think the King wanted Sir Robert to kill a dragon.

Critical Thinking answers will vary. Sample: He might get some food to eat and a place to sleep.

### Mental Images, p. 20

1. Drawings will vary but should show a sea star eating.
2. Drawings will vary but should show a sea star with a mouth on its stomach.

Critical Thinking answers will vary. Sample: It collects food from the bottom of the ocean, so it needs its mouth on the bottom.

### Mental Images, p. 22

2. Answers and drawings will vary. Samples: Beth is having a tea party with some stuffed animals and her kitten; Beth is having a tea party with her toys and her pet.

Critical Thinking answers will vary. Samples: Beth and her friends will eat cookies and drink tea; Beth will invite her friends from school.

### Mental Images, p. 24

1. Answers will vary. Sample: The boy earned a point when he made a goal.
2. Drawings and answers will vary. Sample: Sid scored a goal for the team.

Critical Thinking answers will vary. Sample: Sid's team might have lost the game.

### Prior Knowledge, p. 26

1. Answers will vary. Samples: crow, robin, pigeon, eagle, hawk, sparrow, hummingbird
2. Answers will vary. Samples: Birds can fly; Birds eat worms.
3. Answers will vary. Samples: Birds can use their beaks to open nuts; Birds are the only animals with feathers.

Critical Thinking answers will vary. Sample: I would be an ostrich because they are big birds.

## Answer Key (cont.)

**Prior Knowledge, p. 28**

1. Answers will vary. Samples: pig, horse, chicken, cow

2. Drawings will vary; student should draw a picture of one of the following farm animals: pig, horse, chicken, cow.

Critical Thinking answers will vary. Sample: No, they have to get up early and work hard. OR Yes, because I would love to take care of animals.

**Prior Knowledge, p. 30**

1.–2. Answers will vary. Samples: Bats: mammals, fur, lungs, born alive, drink milk, fly at night, sleep upside down, eat fruit, fish, nectar; Both: fly; breathe air, have wings; Birds: feathers, air sacs, fly during the day, sleep sitting down, eat worms, nuts, and seeds

Critical Thinking answers will vary. Sample: I breath through lungs like bats do.

**Ask Questions, p. 32**

1. Answers will vary. Sample: What can I do to help protect the planet?

2. Answers will vary. Sample: Rosa wanted to keep the dandelions because she liked them.

3. Answers will vary. Sample: Rosa is protecting the rivers and the ocean.

Critical Thinking answers will vary. Sample: I can protect the planet by not throwing trash on the ground and by not wasting water.

**Ask Questions, p. 34**

2. Answers will vary. Samples: Flute: What is it made of?; Drums: How is drum music written?; Guitar: How many strings are on a guitar?; Triangle: Is it easy to play?

Critical Thinking answers will vary. Sample: I would like to play the flute because it has a pretty sound.

## Answer Key (cont.)

### Ask Questions, p. 36

1. Answers will vary. Sample: Who is going to get the surprise?

2. Answers will vary. Sample: What are the kids wrapping?

3. Answers will vary. Sample: How will the gift be used in the garden?

Critical Thinking answers will vary. Sample: They loved her and wanted to do something special for her birthday.

### Make Connections, p. 38

1. Answers will vary. Sample: Ice skates are used to move on ice.

2. Answers will vary. Sample: There was probably a lot of ice where the Vikings lived.

Critical Thinking answers will vary. Sample: They both had blades.

### Make Connections, p. 40

1. Answers will vary. Sample: I celebrate St. Patrick's Day.

2. Answers will vary. Sample: I celebrate Earth Day.

3. Answers will vary. Sample: I eat yummy food and sing songs.

Critical Thinking answers will vary. Sample: No, some people have big parties and some people have small parties with family.

### Make Connections, p. 42

1. Answers will vary. Sample: Yes, because I would teach it tricks.

2. Answers will vary. Sample: She took care of her fish and helped with her baby brother.

3. Drawings will vary but should show the student with a pet. Answers will vary. Sample: friend

Critical Thinking answers will vary. Sample: They didn't have room to keep all of the puppies.

### Setting, p. 44

1. Answers will vary. Sample: The house had a broken window and cobwebs.

2. Drawings will vary but should show an old, scary house. Answers will vary. Sample: The kids hit a ball through the old house's window.

Critical Thinking answers will vary. Sample: No, I wouldn't go into a stranger's house.

## Answer Key (cont.)

### Setting, p. 46

1. Answers will vary. Sample: I will read about a marching band.

2. Answers will vary. Sample: The story takes place on a street.

3. Answers will vary. Sample: It takes place during the day. I know this because most parades take place during the day.

Critical Thinking answers will vary. Sample: They feel proud of Taj because he has worked hard to learn to play an instrument.

### Setting, p. 48

1. Answers will vary. Sample: The setting is on a spaceship in outer space.

2. Drawings will vary but should show a scene in space. Sentences will vary. Sample: The spaceships fly in outer space.

Critical Thinking answers will vary. Sample: They might have been afraid of Grick and Gleep.

### Plot, p. 50

1. Answers will vary. Sample: A genie is supposed to grant wishes.

2. Answers will vary. Sample: The boys find a bottle.

3. Answers will vary. Sample: I wanted to know if there was a genie in it.

Critical Thinking: Lee and Todd would have made wishes.

### Plot, p. 52

1. Answers will vary. Sample: It is a hot day.

2. Answers will vary. Sample: They decide to go swimming.

3. Answers will vary. Sample: There are bees in the backyard.

4. Drawings will vary but should show sprinklers coming on.

Critical Thinking answers will vary. Sample: The girls could have eaten ice cream or played in the sprinklers.

### Plot, p. 54

1. Manny and Jack

2. Answers will vary. Sample: They play together at Manny's house.

3. Answers will vary. Sample: They will play at Manny's house because he doesn't want Jack to feel bad about where he lives.

Critical Thinking answers will vary. Sample: Manny is a kind boy who doesn't want to hurt Jack's feelings.

### Characters, p. 56

2. Answers will vary. Sample: It makes Jo happy to help her mom.

3. Answers will vary. Sample: Jo feels good because she has fun helping her dad and Mrs. Jones gives her a hug.

Critical Thinking answers will vary. Sample: Yes, because it makes me feel good when I help others.

# Answer Key (cont.)

### Characters, p. 58

1. Answers will vary. Sample: Yes, she was funny and liked to play dolls with me.

2. Answers will vary. Sample: No, Adam blames his invisible friend for doing bad things.

3. Answers will vary. Sample: Adam doesn't want to get into trouble.

Critical Thinking answers will vary. Sample: No, because Adam might do bad things and get me into trouble.

### Characters, p. 60

1. Answers will vary. Sample: I will read about a girl going on a trip.

2. Answers will vary. Sample: organized, excited

3. Answers will vary. Sample: Tracy will write about each day of her trip and take pictures.

Critical Thinking answers will vary. Sample: She should pack a sleeping bag, a tent, and a lantern.

### Title and Headings, p. 62

1. Answers will vary. Sample: I will read about different kinds of homes.

2. Answers will vary. Samples: A Tall Home: Apartment buildings have many homes in them; A Painted Home: The home is painted with many different colors; A Dry Home: The roof is made of leaves.

Critical Thinking answers will vary. Sample: My new home would be like a telescope. The home could get taller when more people came over and get shorter when there are just a few people.

### Title and Headings, p. 64

1. Answers will vary. Sample: It will be about shapes in different types of art.

2. Answers will vary. Samples: Shapes in Paintings: The artist uses shapes to make a design or to tell a story; Shapes in Sculptures: Sculptures are made from wood or stone; Shapes in Windows: Stained glass windows have many shapes.

Critical Thinking answers will vary; drawings should use different shapes.

## Answer Key *(cont.)*

### Title and Headings, p. 66

1. Answers will vary. Sample: I will learn how to be healthy.

2. Answers will vary. Samples: Food: Fruits and vegetables help you grow strong; Exercise: Exercise keeps your body healthy; Sleep: It's important to get a good night's sleep.

Critical Thinking answers will vary; drawings should show a healthy activity.

### Typeface and Captions, p. 68

2. Answers will vary. Sample: I learned what to do when crossing the street.

3. Do not; explanations will vary but should tell why these words are boldface. Sample: The words are in boldface so you'll know not to cross the street in the middle.

Critical Thinking answers will vary. Sample: Rules keep us safe because they tell us to not cross the street when cars are coming.

### Typeface and Captions, p. 70

1. Answers will vary. Sample: I will read about sea animals.

2. Drawings should show a sea animal. Answers will vary. Sample: A sea horse is very small.

Critical Thinking answers will vary. Sample: Sea animals live in salty water. Some sea animals are very big and some are very small.

### Typeface and Captions, p. 72

1. Answers will vary. Sample: I will read about shoes.

2. Drawings will vary but should show a type of shoe.

Critical Thinking answers will vary. Sample: My new shoes will have umbrellas on them. When it rains, the umbrellas will pop up and keep my feet dry.

### Graphics, p. 74

1. Answers will vary. Samples: Desert: dry, hot; Prairie: grassy, cold in winter; Rainforest: lots of trees, rainy

2. Drawings will vary but should show a beach scene.

Critical Thinking answers will vary. Sample: I would live in the forest because I like big trees.

### Graphics, p. 76

1. Answers will vary. Sample: I will read about outer space.

2. Answers will vary. Sample: People have changed space by sending up satellites, space stations, and rockets.

3. Drawings will vary but should show some type of space machine.

Critical Thinking answers will vary. Sample: People want to learn about space to know if there is life on other planets.

## Answer Key (cont.)

### Graphics, p. 78

1. Answers will vary. Sample: The pictures show the life cycle of a frog.

2. The frog starts out as an egg, becomes a tadpole, grows legs, and then becomes an adult frog.

3. Drawings should show a frog in some stage of life. Answers will vary. Sample: The tadpole grows legs.

Critical Thinking answers will vary. Sample: If it stayed as a tadpole, it could not live on land.

### Main Idea, p. 80

1. Detective Joe solves mysteries.

2. Answers will vary. Sample: He asked questions. He looked for clues. He went up and down the street.

3. Answers will vary. Sample: Joe used clues that helped him solve the mystery and find the bike.

Critical Thinking answers will vary. Sample: I lost my homework. I had to clean my desk to find it.

### Main Idea, p. 82

1. Drawings will vary but should show weather.

2. Paragraph 1: The weather is all around us; Paragraph 2: Sometimes the weather is good; Paragraph 3: Sometimes the weather is bad.

Critical Thinking answers will vary. Sample: I like rainy weather because I can stay inside and snuggle under a blanket.

### Main Idea, p. 84

1. Answers will vary. Sample: I will read about a new kind of bike.

2. Drawings will vary but should show a bike. Sentences will vary. Sample: The bike can fold in half.

Critical Thinking answers will vary. Sample: The person would not be able to ride the bike.

### Details, p. 86

2. Main Idea: Ben likes to do magic. Details: He has a tall black magic hat. He has a long magic wand.

Critical Thinking answers will vary. Sample: My new trick will make my little brother disappear. My brother will go into a box and poof! He is gone!

**Details, p. 88**

2. Main Idea: In the forest, there are plants.  Details: There are big trees.  There are small flowers.  There are green grasses.

Critical Thinking answers will vary.  Sample: If there weren't any forests, many animals would not have a home.

**Details, p. 90**

2. Main Idea: Robert collects rocks.  Details: He collects big and small rocks.  He collects brown and green rocks.  He collects bumpy rocks and smooth rocks.

Critical Thinking answers will vary.  Sample: I collect teddy bears.  They are cuddly and make good friends.

**Main Idea and Details, p. 92**

1. It is about volcanoes.

2. Answers will vary.  Samples: Main Idea: Volcanoes have a good side.  Details: The ash is good for the ground; Silver and gold are found where lava once was; People heat their homes or water with heat from volcanoes.

Critical Thinking answers will vary.  Sample: The ash makes it hard for people to breathe.  The lava can burn people.

**Main Idea and Details, p. 94**

1. The text is mostly about gravity.

2. Main Idea: Gravity is a force.  Details: It is very strong.  It keeps the moon going around Earth.  It holds us on the ground, too.

Critical Thinking answers will vary.  Sample: People would be floating around.  It would be hard to eat food or drink water.

**Time Order, p. 96**

2. 4, 1, 3, 2, 5

3. Answers will vary.  Samples: birds, alligators, fish

Critical Thinking answers will vary.  Sample: It has to be able to swim right away because that's what turtles naturally know to do.

**Time Order, p. 98**

2. 4, 5, 2, 1, 3, 6

Critical Thinking answers will vary.  Sample: Jan and Bree did subtraction problems in class.

**Time Order, p. 100**

1. Answers will vary.  Sample: It is about airplanes.

2. 4, 2, 3, 1

3. Drawings will vary but should show an airplane from long ago.

Critical Thinking answers will vary.  Sample: Today, planes fly all over the world, but most planes long ago didn't fly far.

**Logical Order, p. 102**

2. 4, 2, 6, 1, 3, 5

Critical Thinking answers will vary. Sample: Luis liked singing and thought he could do well.

**Logical Order, p. 104**

1. first, next, then, soon, then

2. 3, 4, 1, 2

Critical Thinking answers will vary. Sample: I get out the toothpaste and my toothbrush. I put toothpaste on the toothbrush. I brush my teeth.

**Logical Order, p. 106**

1. Answers will vary. Sample: I will learn about skateboard tricks.

2. 4, 2, 5, 1, 3

Critical Thinking answers will vary. Sample: I will get the skateboard rolling, jump up, and then land back down on the skateboard.

**Retell, p. 108**

1. Answers will vary. Sample: Tigers are cats. Tigers like to swim. A tiger's stripes help it hide. At night, tigers hunt for food.

2. Drawings will vary but should show a tiger.

Critical Thinking answers will vary. Sample: They both are cats and have fur and claws.

**Retell, p. 110**

2. Answers will vary. Sample: A man in England bought a metal detector. He used it to find coins and other metal things. He found treasures. Experts came to look at the things he found.

Critical Thinking answers will vary. Sample: We can learn about how people used to live, what they made, and what they wore.

**Retell, p. 112**

1. Answers will vary. Sample: Cat and Mouse are friends. They live in the same house. They both eat people food, chase toys, and take naps.

2. Drawings will vary but should show a cat and a mouse.

Critical Thinking answers will vary. Sample: At first, the cat and dog would not like each other. Then they would become good friends.

**Cause and Effect, p. 114**

1. Effects: The pieces of land push against each other; This rock can melt; Then it is called lava.

Critical Thinking answers will vary. Sample: I might be late for school and make my parents late for work.

### Cause and Effect, p. 116

1. Answers will vary. Samples: Effects: Marty and his dad decide to go to the store; He couldn't start the car; The door would not open; Marty climbed through the window and got the keys.

Critical Thinking answers will vary. Sample: They would not be able to get into the house to get the keys.

### Compare and Contrast, p. 118

1. Answers will vary. Sample: They would both be fun places to visit.

2. Answers will vary. Samples: See: a play, hills; Do: ride the subway, ride horses; Sleep: in a hotel; by a campfire

Critical Thinking answers will vary. Sample: I would like to go to a city because I would like to ride on a subway.

### Compare and Contrast, p. 120

1. Answers will vary. Sample: ladybugs: eat aphids, keep plants healthy and strong; both: helpful, bugs; bees: sip nectar, make honey

Critical Thinking answers will vary. Sample: I think bees are more helpful because they make honey that people can eat.

### Author's Purpose, p. 122

1. The author is writing about apples and oranges.

2. Answers will vary. Sample: The author wants the reader to think that apples are better than oranges.

3. Answers will vary. Sample: No, because I have always loved apples.

Critical Thinking answers will vary. Sample: Yes, because apples come in beautiful colors and they taste good. OR No, because I like juicy oranges better.

### Author's Purpose, p. 124

1. Answers will vary. Sample: Clocks and calendars measure time. In the past, people did not have clocks or calendars. People used the sun and the moon to keep track of time.

2. Answers will vary. Sample: The author wants to give information about measuring time.

3. Answers will vary. Sample: I use a calendar to keep track of the days.

Critical Thinking answers will vary. Sample: People will have robots that will tell them the time.

## Answer Key (cont.)

**Table of Contents, p. 126**

1. The book is about a visit to a farm.

2. Answers will vary. Sample: I can see which chapters are in the book and what I will be reading about.

3. Answers will vary. Sample: The table of contents also has the page number for each chapter.

Critical Thinking answers will vary. Samples: There could be a chapter on tractors; There could be a chapter about all of the types of tools that farmers use on a farm.

**Table of Contents, p. 128**

1. Answers will vary. Sample: I would add "Tricks to Teach Your Horse."

2. Drawings will vary but should show a horse working on a farm, pulling a cart in a city, rounding up cattle, etc. Sentences will vary. Sample: The horse plows the field.

Critical Thinking answers will vary. Sample: I would like to read about dogs because I want a dog for a pet.

**Index, p. 130**

1. This book is about firefighters.

2. The index is in ABC order.

3. 11, 15

Critical Thinking answers will vary. Sample: I can use an index to find information on a special topic in a book.

**Index, p. 132**

1. Africa, Australia, Spain, United Kingdom

2. Answers will vary. Sample: bread, cheese, churros

3. pages 4, 9, 11

Critical Thinking answers will vary. Sample: I would make an index about snacks. I would include page numbers for ice cream, fruits and vegetables, cookies, and crackers.

**Glossary, p. 134**

1. The glossary gives the meanings of words.

2. Answers will vary. Sample: No, because these words are for a book about Canada.

Critical Thinking: A glossary gives the meaning of words in the book, and an index tells what topics are in a book.

**Glossary, p. 136**

1. Answers will vary. Sample: crust—top layer of the earth

2. Answers will vary. Sample: These words are listed in the glossary because they are important in understanding earthquakes.

Critical Thinking answers will vary. Sample: A glossary and a dictionary both have words and their meanings.

# Contents of the Teacher Resource CD

| Skill | Filename |
|---|---|
| **Preview** | |
| *Brad's Kittens* | page008.pdf<br>page009.pdf |
| *All About Horses* | page010.pdf<br>page011.pdf |
| *What Is a Map?* | page012.pdf<br>page013.pdf |
| **Predict** | |
| *The Loose Tooth* | page014.pdf<br>page015.pdf |
| *Liz's Wishes* | page016.pdf<br>page017.pdf |
| *Sir Robert* | page018.pdf<br>page019.pdf |
| **Mental Images** | |
| *Snacking with Sea Stars* | page020.pdf<br>page021.pdf |
| *Tea Anyone?* | page022.pdf<br>page023.pdf |
| *Goal!* | page024.pdf<br>page025.pdf |
| **Prior Knowledge** | |
| *Bird Talk* | page026.pdf<br>page027.pdf |
| *Pat's Farm* | page028.pdf<br>page029.pdf |
| *Bats Are Not Birds* | page030.pdf<br>page031.pdf |
| **Ask Questions** | |
| *Protect the Planet* | page032.pdf<br>page033.pdf |
| *The School Band* | page034.pdf<br>page035.pdf |
| *The Surprise* | page036.pdf<br>page037.pdf |
| **Make Connections** | |
| *Viking Ice Skates* | page038.pdf<br>page039.pdf |
| *Holidays* | page040.pdf<br>page041.pdf |
| *Free Puppies* | page042.pdf<br>page043.pdf |

| Skill | Filename |
|---|---|
| **Setting** | |
| *The House* | page044.pdf<br>page045.pdf |
| *The Marching Band* | page046.pdf<br>page047.pdf |
| *The Spaceship* | page048.pdf<br>page049.pdf |
| **Plot** | |
| *Genie in a Bottle* | page050.pdf<br>page051.pdf |
| *Buzzing Bees* | page052.pdf<br>page053.pdf |
| *The New Kid* | page054.pdf<br>page055.pdf |
| **Characters** | |
| *Thank You, Jo!* | page056.pdf<br>page057.pdf |
| *The Invisible Friend* | page058.pdf<br>page059.pdf |
| *Tracy's Trip* | page060.pdf<br>page061.pdf |
| **Title and Headings** | |
| *Homes* | page062.pdf<br>page063.pdf |
| *Shapes in Art* | page064.pdf<br>page065.pdf |
| *Staying Healthy* | page066.pdf<br>page067.pdf |
| **Typeface and Captions** | |
| *Rules for Crossing the Street* | page068.pdf<br>page069.pdf |
| *Sea Life* | page070.pdf<br>page071.pdf |
| *Super Shoes* | page072.pdf<br>page073.pdf |
| **Graphics** | |
| *Land* | page074.pdf<br>page075.pdf |
| *People and Outer Space* | page076.pdf<br>page077.pdf |
| *A Frog's Life* | page078.pdf<br>page079.pdf |

# Contents of the Teacher Resource CD *(cont.)*

# Notes

#50724—*Read and Succeed: Comprehension Level 1* © *Shell Education*